Anonymus

Tenth Annual Report

Alabama Institution for the Education of the Deaf, Dumb and Blind

Anonymus

Tenth Annual Report
Alabama Institution for the Education of the Deaf, Dumb and Blind

ISBN/EAN: 9783741177798

Manufactured in Europe, USA, Canada, Australia, Japa

Cover: Foto ©Thomas Meinert / pixelio.de

Manufactured and distributed by brebook publishing software
(www.brebook.com)

Anonymus

Tenth Annual Report

TENTH ANNUAL REPORT

—OF THE—

BOARD OF COMMISSIONERS AND OFFICERS

—OF THE—

ALABAMA INSTITUTION

—FOR THE—

EDUCATION OF THE DEAF, DUMB & BLIND,

For the Year 1870.

TO HIS EXCELLENCY W. H. SMITH, THE GOVERNOR.

————◄◆►————

MONTGOMERY, ALA.:
JOHN G. STOKES & CO., STATE PRINTERS.
1870.

DEAF AND DUMB ALPHABET.

a a	b b	c c	d d	e e

f f	g g	h h	i i	j j

k k	l l	m m	n n	o o

p p	q q	r r	s s	t t

u u	v v	w w	x x	y y

z z	& &

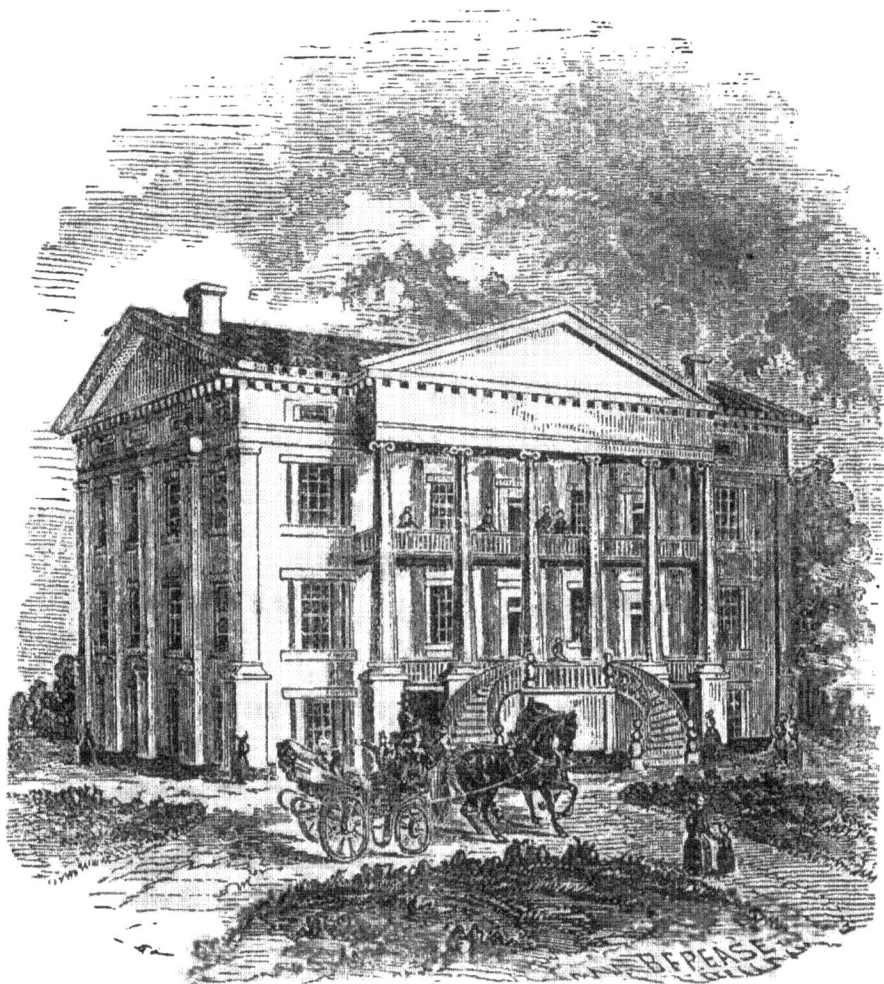

Alabama Institution for the Deaf, Dumb and Blind,
AT TALLADEGA.

BOARD OF COMMISSIONERS:

M. H. CRUIKSHANK,	Talladega
WM. TAYLOR,	"
GEO. S. WALDEN,	"
A. G. STORY,	"
A. BINGHAM,	"
G. T. McAFEE,	"
CHAS. PELHAM,	"
N. B. CLOUD,	Montgomery.
WM. H. SMITH,	"

OFFICERS OF THE BOARD:

M. H. CRUIKSHANK,	President.
A. G. STORY,	Treasurer.
J. H. JOHNSON,	Secretary.

AUDITING COMMITTEE:

GREEN T. McAFEE.   WM. TAYLOR,

OFFICERS OF THE INSTITUTION:

J. H. JOHNSON,	Principal.
MR. REUBEN R. ASBURY,	Instructor of the Blind.
MRS. EMILY A. JOHNSON,	Teacher of Mutes.
MR. JEHU A. HODGE,	Teacher of Mutes.
MISS EMMA OMBERG,	Teacher of Music.
MRS. C. B. ASBURY,	Matron.
MRS. E. J. GROOM,	House-Keeper.

PHYSICIAN:
J. H. JOHNSON, M. D.

CONSULTING PHYSICIAN:
DR. J. C. KNOX.

REPORT.

*Office of the Board of Commissioners of the Alabama Institu-
tion for the Deaf, Dumb, and Blind.*

TALLADEGA, ALA., }
October 25, 1870. }

To his Excellency Wm. H. Smith, Governor of Alabama:

SIR : In accordance with the requirement of the law establishing this institution, I have the honor to submit herewith the tenth annual report of th Board of Commissioners and officers of the Alabama Institution for the Deaf and Dumb and the Blind.

I would respectfully call the attention of your Excellency to the report of the Improvement Committee, to whom was entrusted the re-roofing of the main building, repairs, &c., upon the premises, and the purchase of a piano for the use of the blind pupils. The suggestions of the committee meet the hearty approval of the board, and it is hoped will meet the approbation of your Excellency. The report of the Principal, who acts also as Secretary of the Board, sets forth in full the progress and present condition of the institution. To it, I respectfully refer you for details.

Very respectfully, your obedient servant,

M. H. CRUIKSHANK, President.

REPORT OF PRINCIPAL.

ALABAMA INSTITUTION FOR DEAF, DUMB AND BLIND, {
October 25th, 1870. }

To the Board of Commissioners:

GENTLEMEN: The record of the past year in the history of this institution is one of uninterrupted prosperity. The Giver of all Good has dealt bountifully with us ; "goodness and mercy" hath followed us ; no serious illness nor accident has occured ; on the other hand, many of our pupils who came to us from unhealthy localities, saturated with malaria, have been restored to health, and their pale cheeks made to bloom with health. Each succeeding year demonstrates the wisdom of the choice made by the founders of the institution, in the selection of its location. The whole number of pupils in attendance since date of last report is :

Whole number of pupils........................ 55
Number of mutes............................ 41
Number of blind............................ 14— 55
Numbers of males............................ 16
Number of females............................ 39— 55

A catalogue of the names of the pupils is appended to this report. The progress of the pupils has, upon the whole, been satisfactory, though, more than ever before, we have labored under the great disadvantage of having the time of our teachers divided between a number of classes. It seems to be impossible to make the parents and friends of the pupils sensible of the necessity of bringing them to the institution at the opening of the term. I must, therefore, *again urge upon* the board, to make it a *rule*, not to be varied from, except for good and sufficient reason, to refuse admission to *all* who fail to be in attendance by the close of the second week of the term. There are at this time on the register of the institution the names of (61) sixty-one pupils who have applied for admission, and of this number there are only twenty-six mutes and seven blind pupils who have come promptly at the opening of school—only a little over half of those who, in all probability, will be here before the close of the quarter. We shall, in consequence of this neglect, on the part of parents, be compelled to secure the services of another teacher or fail in our duty towards those who have been prompt. Another reason why we shall be forced to secure additional aid in the mute department is, that we have one pupil, a *girl*, totally deaf and dumb and almost entirely blind, who can be taught neither in a class of mutes nor blind pupils, but must, to do her justice, have the greater portion of the time of a teacher. She is intelligent, and exceedingly anxious to learn. Her case appeals more directly perhaps than does that of any other in the institution, to the benevolence of the State, and to the sympathies of all charitable people. We have information of another and similar case, not yet old enough to enter the institution. I mention this here, not in order that you, gentlemen, who know all about the wants and necessities of the institution, but that the legislature and the public may know something of the demands upon us as a State charity.

It has been our earnest desire, and we have made every effort in our power, both by correspondence and through the press of the State, to make known, as far as we possibly could, the provision made by the State for the education of its deaf mute, and blind children. We have met with some degree of success, but by far the larger number of these unfortunate children *are kept* at their homes, growing up in ignorance and darkness. Ought this so to be? We have said *kept* at home, and we think the figures on one of the foregoing pages of this report will prove that this is so. These figures show the whole number of pupils to have been fifty-five; of this number, only sixteen were boys, and of *this* small number, I have to add that seven of them were blind, leaving only *nine* mute boys out of *the whole* number in the State of *Alabama* who have been *allowed* to go to school. It is well known, that no such disproportion as this exists, as to the number of each sex. Before the war our pupils were about equally divided—boys, and girls. I append to this report a list of the institutions for the instruction of the deaf and dumb in the United States, showing the number of pupils in each, and the number of males and females. No such disparity exists, except in one institution, the Catholic of St. Louis, and I venture to assert, from a like cause, namely: "The boys make *good field hands,* and they are not sent to school because *they* don't *know* what they are losing, and their friends (?) keep them at home for their labor. Without education, the deaf mute can only be a day laborer, know nothing of his moral responsibility, is not competent to *conduct business* for himself ; and if he be poor, must sooner or later become a burden upon his friends or the *public.* Educate him, and you return him to society an intelligent, valuable and self-supporting citizen. The *State* has been ful y up to her duty in providing the means of education. Is there no way to induce the attendance of the pupils ?

As to the blind, we think it is only necessary for the benevolent provision made by the State for their benefit to become generally known and understood, to secure the attendance of almost all of that class.

BLIND DEPARTMENT.

Since the date of the last report, this department has been permanently established in connection with that for the deaf and dumb. By legislative enactment the name of the institution was changed. It is now called, "The Alabama Institution for the Deaf and Dumb and the Blind." The act referred to, adds five thousand dollars annually to the appropriation for the support of the instition, making the appropriation received now by the institution, thirteen thousand dollars per annum. In addition to this, the legislature appropriated *three* thousand dollars, as a special appropriation, for re-roofing the building, making some repairs on the premises, and to purchase musical instruments for the use of the blind pupils. The report of the Improvement Coommittee, herewith submitted, will show what disposition has been made of this fund. The act also provided for the addition of four *members* to the Board of Commissioners, the Governor of the State, ex-officio, together with Messrs. G. T. McAffee, Arthur Bingham and Charles Pelham, appointed by the Governor, compose the four additional members.

These gentlemen have entered upon the discharge of their duty as members of the board, and have cordially co-operated with us in our efforts to advance the interests of the institution.

MUSIC DEPARTMENT.

This department has been organized by the appointment of Miss E. Omberg, an accomplished and thorough teacher of several years experience, who has entered upon the discharge of her duties enthusiastically. We have one of "Knabe's" best Pianos, made expressly for us, and strengthened to withstand school-room usage. Our success in this department, we think, is assured, from the anxiety of the pupils to learn, and the ability and industry of the teacher in instructing them.

MECHANICAL DEPARTMENT.

In this department, we encounter more difficulties than in any other. This is to be regretted the more, because the benefit to the pupils of a *good* trade, is *only* second to his *mental* development. There are various things which restrict us in the selection of branches of handicraft taught in our institutions of this kind. The first and most important is, that the trade taught must be one requiring but a small outlay of capital for tools and materials. This restricts us, as will be seen, by consulting the list appended to their report, showing the trades taught at the different institutions in the United States, to a very few branches of industry that can be successfully carried on. Shoe and boot making for the mutes, and broom making and cane work for the blind, are the branches taught in this institution. We have done but little in this department; 1st. for the want of shop room; 2d. because we cannot compete in prices with regular manufactories, and buy the materials; and consumers do not like to have their materials worked up by beginners. It is, therefore, impossible to make the shops self-sustaining, and we have heretofore been too much straitened for means to afford to run the shop all the time. We think, though, if we can get the means to erect a good shop building and sale-room, and equip it with some modern machinery, so as to enable us to keep one or two regular hands employed on custom work, that we can then make the shops *pay out*, and have all the boys well taught.

As to our female pupils, aside from ordinary sewing and house work, we have done nothing towards teaching the mute girls. The blind girls have been taught by the matron *to do* bead work, and some of them have succeeded most admirably in this accomplishment, which, although it be but an accomplishment, will enable many of them to do something towards supporting themselves after they leave school. There are experiments being made in the northern institutions with the sewing and knitting machines, which promise well. I have a communication from a blind lady in Philadelphia, in which she states that she has made herself familiar with the working of several of the best sewing machines, and finds that blind *girls can* be taught the use of the sewing machine to advantage. We propose, whenever we are able to so, to try this experiment.

To enable us, though, to do anything more than we are now doing, we must be provided with the means to erect a suitable shop for the male pupils, with sales-room attached, for the storage and sale of our material and manufactured articles. I have visited during the summer the shops in the best conducted northern schools, and can secure the aid of the managers of those shops, in fitting up a shop in the most approved style. I, therefore, respectfully ask that application be made to the legislature at its next session, for an appropriation to secure this much desired addition to our institution.

OUT-BUILDINGS AND FENCES.

Our barn, stable and cow-house, is an old, dilapidated and insecure structure, wholly inadequate for our purposes; we very much need a new one. The fencing around the premises is about half of it in good order; the fund for improvements having been exhausted before we had more than half finished repairing the fences. We are now negotiating for a safe and cheap apparatus for lighting our buildings. The outlay for the gas machine and piping, may be considerable, but as the safety of the inmates and buildings depends upon having a *safe light*, and as the difference in the cost of the light proposed and the *candles* we now use, will pay for the new machine and piping in a few years, we think economy, as well as prudence, dictates the expenditure. Painting of end blinds to the main building, *wardrobes* for the pupils, clothes, and some chamber and dining room furniture, are also much needed to complete the accommodations of the institution. I respectfully call your attention to the report of Dr. Taylor, one of your own body, as to his observations in the Indiana institutions for the Deaf and Dumb and Blind, made during a visit the past summer, to those admirably conducted institutions.

The foregoing embraces all that I have to say at this time in reference to the affairs of the institution. Full statements as to receipts and disbursements, with reports from the treasurer and improvement committee, together with estimates for the proposed improvements, will be found appended to this report.

In conclusion, gentlemen, I beg to return my sincere thanks to you for the uniform kindness extended to me by you, and for the confidence reposed and assistance given me in the management of the affairs of the institution. Committing the institution to your fostering care for another year, and commending it and all its interests to a merciful Providence,

I have the honor to be,

Your most obedient servant,

JOS. H. JOHNSON,
Principal.

October 25th, 1870.

Hon. M. H. Cruikshank, President Board of Commissioners of the Alabama Institute for the Deaf and Dumb and Blind—

SIR: The earnest and liberal manifestation of your body in the cause of deaf, mute and blind education, in delegating your principal, Dr. Jos. H. Johnson and myself to the convention of the representatives of the deaf, mute and blind educators of North America, which assembled at Indianapolis on the 29th of August last, was responded to on the part of your delegates, with a consciousness of the importance of the trust reposed in them.

Accordingly, in obedience to your instructions, your representatives attended that convention, to witness and participate in its deliberations, to hear the different systems of instruction and discipline discussed, and to note what progress had been made in the great and almost holy labor of elevating the mental, moral and social condition of the deaf and dumb, and the blind—those unfortunate children of "silence and darkness."

The convention was largely attended—embracing in its body, men of distinguished ability, zeal and philanthropy—with representatives from Louisiana to Minnesota, and from Nova Scotia to California. No attempt will be made in this brief report, to give even a synopsis of its deliberations. It is sufficient for the present, to say that your delegates were much profited by what they saw and heard, since the convention discussed to a greater or less extent, almost every subject within the range of deaf, mute education.

Your delegates, however, cannot dismiss the subject, without acknowledging their profound obligations to Mr. Thomas Macintyre, the distinguished superintendent of the Indiana institute for the deaf and dumb, for hospitable and courteous attention; to Mr. W.H. Churchman, the thorough and efficient superintendent of the Indiana blind institute, they are likewise indebted for kind attention; and to Mr. Bryce M. Patton, of the Kentucky blind institute, and to Mr. P. G. Gillett, the talented and indefatigable superintendent of the Illinois institution for the Deaf and Dumb, they are further indebted for kind favors and attentions. These several institutions were visited and inspected by your delegates.

But in visiting these liberally endowed and thoroughly appointed institutions, your delegates could not fail to be forcibly impressed with the fact, that the Alabama institute, in those particulars, was much less fortunate. If the interest which a State manifests in educating, developing, humanizing. perfecting and elevating the more unfortunate class of its citizens, is to be taken as the measure of its

civilization, Alabama would fall far short of many of her
sister States. While her general school system was well
conceived, and her educational fund ample, the appropriation for the establishmert of the institute for the deaf and
dumb and blind, and the support thereof, have not been
commensurate with the importance which the subject demands.

This institution was organized and put in operation and
is sustained at the expense of the State, for the purpose of
educating, ameliorating and elevating the condition of all
the deaf and dumb and blind, of suitable ages, to be found
within her borders. Yet but a moiety of these classes
have ever entered the institution. The census of 1850,
shows that there were in the State at that period, 210
deaf mutes, and 295 blind, making an aggregate number
of more than 500 of these unfortunate people. Of this
number, it is but fair to estimate that fully one-half (250),
come within the educational ages; and although we have
as yet no means of ascertaining the result of the census of
1870, on those points, it is almost certain that the number has not diminished, but possibly, a considerable increase
will be shown. But in the face of these facts, it is mani-
fest from the report of the principal, that but 55 pupils
have at any one session made application for admission,
and that not above 40 have actually entered the classes
of the institution. This is a startling announcement, and
evinces a criminal neglect on the part of the parents or
guardians, for which a remedy should be provided.

Finally, Mr. President, as a member of your "building
committee," I am not inclined to take leave of this subject, without urging upon your attention the necessity of
further appropriations for the improvement and repairs of
the grounds and buildings of the institution. The commissioners are the legal custodians of the interests of the
institute, and are responsible for its preservation and come-

liness, and in some measure for its success; but without the requisite support from the State, little can be accomplished in that direction. You are aware, that further repairs and improvements are actually needed, and cannot be wisely deferred.

The means of ingress and egress to and from the building, are wholly inadequate to the demands. The temporary wooden steps placed there years ago, are fast falling into decay, and will soon become useless. These should be replaced by steps constructed of iron or stone, or other durable material ; and should bear some proportion in fitness, to the size and style of the building.

The windows have never been provided with *blinds*, which are much needed for the comfort and protection of the inmates. The saving in the item of curtains alone, would soon pay the costs of the blinds.

For a period of nearly twenty years, no painting has been done about the building, and many parts of it, the cornice especially, is damaging materially for want of this trifling expenditure. The kitchen and out-houses, too, being wooden structures, are sadly in need of paint.

These are but a part of the repairs and improvements, which ought to receive immediate attention. Others are doubtless apparent to your own mind. The institution was not established for the present generation alone. It was intended to be permanent, and to transmit its humane and beneficient influence to our posterity of future ages. We could wish to see it increase in beauty and usefulness, and become as imperishable as the mountains, whose blue-waiving outlines encircle the beautiful and salubrious valley in which it is situated.

Trusting, therefore, that you will appeal to the legislature for such an appropriation as shall be ample to make all the additional improvements that may be necessary to

place the grounds and buildings in thorough repair, and
that your appeal will not be made in vain.

I have the honor to remain, very truly,

Your obedient servant,

W. TAYLOR.

Talladega, Oct. 31st, 1870.

REPORT OF IMPROVEMENT COMMITTEE.

To the Board of Commissioners :

GENTLEMEN: Your committee, to whom was entrusted
the improvements made upon the building and premises of
the institution, and the purchase of musical instruments
for the use of the blind pupils, beg leave to make the fol-
lowing report :

And first, as the matter of the greatest importance, your
committee decided to re-roof the *main* building with slate,
which has been done in a most substantial manner. The
slate was procured from the Polk county Georgia quarries -
cost of the same on the yard, 8 dollars per square ; the va l
leys and gutters are made of the best sheet copper, weigh-
ing one pound to the square foot. *The* wood parapets and
copings are substantially covered with tin, and painted.
The frame work of the roof was repaired and strengthened
and the old sheating thrown off and replaced by good,
square-edged inch thick lumber. The whole job, done under the superintendence of Mr. E. G. Morris, one of the
best mechanics in the State. The slate-work was done under the direction of Mr. M. E. Jones of Atlanta, Georgia,
a workman thoroughly acquainted with his business. The
cost of slate, hauling, freight, lumber, wages, &c., can be
seen by examining the subjoined account of the disburse-
ment of improvement fund.

The erection of a wood building, containing ironing rooms for the girls, bath rooms and servants sleeping rooms, were paid for in part out of the improvement fund, and is charged up on the same account. The repairing of the fences, as far as it has been done, is also included.

The committee concluded, at present, to purchase only one piano, and we have given the preference to Messrs. "Knabe" of Baltimore, who made us a very liberal deduction on the price of one of their best 7-octave rosewood instruments, strengthened for school room use.

After all these expenditures, which includes everything due on account of improvements, except a small bill not yet paid for painting, there is left in hands of the treas-urer the sum of $145 86.

All of which is respectfully submitted.

WM. H. CRUIKSHANK,

JOS. H. JOHNSON,

WM. TAYLOR,

Committee.

18

ACKNOWLEDGMENTS.

We take great pleasure and pride in acknowledging the many acts of kindness shown us, by generous friends and the public press during the past year. Our thanks are due to Dr. S. G. Howe of Boston, for a copy of the "Old Curiosity Shop," printed in raised letters, at the author's expense, and distributed free of charge to the blind of the United States by Dr. Howe. Also to Col. C. T. Pollard, President of the Mobile and Montgomery Railroad, Montgomery and West Point Railroad and the Western Railroad. for free passes over those roads, to the Principal of the institution. This generosity on the part of Col. P., will enable us to canvas those portions of the State traversed by said roads, in search of those unfortunate ones who ought to be brought into the institution.

We have applied for, and hope to receive, similar favors from other roads in the State.

We are duly sensible, and return our sincere thanks to the press of the State, for the interest they have manifested and the many kind notices given of our efforts to amelieorate the condition of the deaf mutes and the blind of Alabama.

TERMS OF ADMISSION.

Beneficiaries of the State are received into the institution, free of charge for board and tuition. The parents or friends must furnish neat comfortable clothing, or deposit the money to purchase them with the Steward, They must also pay their traveling expenses to and from the institution. Pay pupils charged two hundred dollars for school year of forty weeks, until further orders from the board.

No pupil of known bad character, or one who has any contageous disease, admitted.

The term opens on the first Monday in Uctober, and continues forty weeks.

JOS. H. JOHNSON, *Principal.*

INDIGENT PUPILS—HOW ADMITTED.

As a matter of convenience to those who may desire to send indigent pupils to the institution, we copy in full the eighth section of the act of the 27th of January, 1860, establishing the institution :

" *Be it further enacted*, That the main object of the institution shall be to afford the means of education to the indigent deaf and dumb and blind of the State. Application for admission must be make to the Board of Commissioners in writing, and must state their name, age, place of birth and present residence, how long the applicant has been a resident of this State, that he or she is deaf and dumb or blind, that the applicant, or his or her family, are unable to pay his or her board and tuition. This application must be sworn to by the applicant, or by some one cognisant of the facts. and filed with the board. Whereupon the board shall, if they deem the proof sufficient, cause an order to be entered on the record of their proceedings, admitting said applicant, a certified copy o which shall be delivered to the applicant or his or he parent, guardian or friend, who shall thereupon be admit ted as a member of said institution, for the period of time specified in the certificate. '

TLIS OF NEWSPAPERS SENT TO THE INSTITUTION, FREE OF
CHARGE, DURING THE PAST YEAR.

1. *Montgomery Advertiser,*   Daily, Montgomery, Ala.
2. *State Journal,*   "   "
3. *Rome Daily,*   "   Rome, Geo.
4. *Mountain Home,*   Weekly, Talladega, Ala.
5. *Rising Star,*   "   Oxford.
6. *Shelby Guide,*   "   Columbiana,
7. *Marion Commonwealth,*   "   Marion,
8. *Union Springs Times,*   "   Union Springs,
9. *Selma Argus,*   "   Selma,
10. *Talladega Watchtower,*   "   Talladega,
11. *Alabama Reporter,*   "   "
12. *Elyton Sun,*   "   Elyton,
13. *The Sun,*   "   Talladega.

The proprietors of the above papers have placed us under renewed obligations, by sending us, each of them, a copy of their journal free of cost. Our thanks are especially due the Messrs. Mosely, who, though not now citizens of our State, have sent us a copy of each of their three papers—one a daily.

ESTIMATE FOR 1871.

For support of sixty pupils..........$15,600 $15,600
For shops and tools.................. 5,000
Fencing and working on grounds..... 1,000
Furniture and beds.................. 1,000
Barn................................ 700
Front steps......................... 300   10,000

$25,600

CATALOGUE OF PUPILS.

Names.	Residence.
1. Mary E. Toney,	Bullock county, Alabama.
2. Georgia Toney,	" "
3. Laura Toney,	" "
4. Maria C. Mims,	Autauga county, Ala.
5. Mary A. Wakefield,	Calhoun county, Ala.
6. Sarah J. Wakefield,	" "
7. Josephine Malear,	Tallapoosa county, Ala
8. Delelah Malear,	" "
9. Elvira Elrod,	Calhoun county, Ala.
10. Sarah J. Steward,	" "
11. Emma McCaine,	Clay, county, Ala
12. Virginia McCaine,	" "
13. Jane House,	Cherokee county, Ala.
14. James House,	" "
15. Asa Stephens,	Blount county, Ala.
16. Mary C. Christian,	Perry county, Ala.
17. Jas. W. Storey,	Greene county, Ala.
18. Beulah Holsomback,	Shelby county, Ala.
19. Georgia C. Whitman,	Perry county, Ala.
20. L. B. Moore,	Pike county, Ala.
21. Ella Zee Groom,	Wilcox county, Ala.
22. Sarah Morgan,	" "
23. Jane Morgan,	" "
24. Algerenia Morgan,	" "
25. Mary E. Mynatt,	Talladega county, Ala.
26. Jane Steed,	Cleburne county, Ala.
27. Martha Trucks,	Bibb county, Ala.
28. Laura Lineberger,	Pickens county, Ala.
29. Jennie Owens,	Butler county, Ala.
30. Martha A. Watson	Calhoun county, Ala.
31. Willie Harriss,	Montgomery county, Ala.

Names.	Residence.
32. Osceola Roberts,	Shelby county, Alabama.
33. Smith Williams,,	Pickens county, Ala.
34. M. A. E. Cowsert,	" "
35. Francis P. Doherty,	Mobile county, Ala.
36. John D. Briscoe,	Jackson county, Ala.
37. Georgia E. Payne,	Tallapoosa county, Ala.
38. Louisa C. Cardinal,	Montgomery county, Ala.
39. John F. Hughes,	Pickens county, Ala.
40. Sarah Jane Wilson,	Randolph county, Ala.
41. Martha E. Dickey,	Montgomery county, Ala.
42. Robert Tims,	St. Clair county, Ala.
43. William McCormick,	Tallapoosa county, Ala.
44. Lamar Knox,	Talladega county, Ala.
45. Frank White,	Pickens county, Ala.
46. William McKeever,	Mobile county, Ala.
47. Richard Cox,	St. Clair county, Ala.
48. Henry Cox,	" "
49. Jane Cox,	" "
50. Elizabeth Dickinson,	Talladega county, Ala.
51. Sarah Fisher,	Mobile county, Ala.
52. Fanny Sims,	Tallapoosa county, Ala.
53. Alice Davis,	Etowah county, Ala.
54. Julia Davis,	" "
55. Martha McClinton,	Shelby county, Ala.

Improvement Committee, in account with the Alabama Institution for the Deaf and Dumb and Blind:

1870.   DR.

March 16. To amount placed in hands
of the treasurer, Col. A.
G. Story, subject to our
draft $3,000 00

CR.

By amount paid for piano, $105 62
"   "   "   " lumber,   571 51
"   "   "   " slate..   592 20
"   "   "   " hauling
slate 157 50
" amount paid for freight
on slate............   61 35
" amount paid for copper
and tin... ....   236 70
" amount paid M.E.Jones,
slater.............   74 50
" amount paid for copper
and tin work, paints,
nails, &c...........   204 57
" amount paid for labor
and wages. 550 19 $2,854 14

" amount in hands of treas-
urer $145 86

                                $3,000 00

Examined, audited and found correct.

                    G. T. MCAFEE,
                    WM. TAYLOR,
                        Auditing Committee.

Jos. H. Johnson, principal, in account with the Alabama Institution for the deaf and dumb and the blind, from October 3, 1869, to July 4th, 1870.

1869.   DR.

July   3. To amount in hand this day, $293 62
"   "   "   "   advanced on 3d
                  quarter, 1869 ...... 700 00
Nov. 11. " amount warrant of this
                  date 1,000 00
1870.
Jan.   3. To amount warrant of this
                  date 1,718 91
March 16. " amount received from
                  A. G. Story, treasurer, 500 00
April 27. " amount received from
                  A. G. Story, treasur'r 3,339 03
July   4. " amount received from
                  A. G. Story, treasur'r 3,500 00

Whole amount received....... $11,051 56
1870.   CR.
       By amount of expenses 3d
                  quarter, 1869...... $919 24
Jan.   3. " amount quarterly set-
                  tlement...........   2,787 65
April 2. " amount quarterly set-
                  tlement...........   3,063 52
June 25.   4,436 06
Oct. 25. " amount due me balance, $154 91

                              $11,206 47–$11,206 47

Audited and found correct.

                    G. T. McAFEE,
                    WM. TAYLOR,
                    Auditing Committee.

MONTGOMERY, ALABAMA.

N. B. Cloud, Treasurer, in account with Alabama Institution for deaf, damb and blind, from October 4th, 1869, to January 3d, 1870.

1869.   DR.

Oct. 4. To amount of warrant drawn
         on the Comptroller in favor
         of Jos. H. Johnson, princi-
         pal...................... $1,046 94

Nov. 11. To amount of warrant drawn
         on the Comptroller in fa-
         vor of Jos. H. Johnston,
         principal.............. 1,000 00

1870.

Jan. 3. To amount of warrant drawn
         on the Comptroller in fa-
         vor or Jos. H. Johnson,
         principal............. 1,718 91
                              _____
                              $4,665 85

The above account was made out from the institution record book, and shows the exact amount drawn from the treasury since date of last report and up to the date of March 8th, 1870, which begins Col. Story's account as treasurer.

TALLADEGA, ALABAMA.

A. G. Storey, treasurer, in account with Alabama institution for the deaf, dumb and blind, from March 16th to July 4th, 1870.

1870.

To amount received from State treasurer on my warrant, dated March 8th, 1870............................ 500 00

To amount received from State treasurer on my warrant, dated April 13th, 1870...........................3,339 03

To amount received from State treasurer on my warrant, dated June 28th, 1870...........................3,500 00

$7,339 03

March 16. By amount paid M. H. Cruikshank, President, draft in favor of Jos. H. Johnson, principal.......... 500 00

April 27. By amount paid M. H. Cruikshank, President, draft in favor of Jos. H. Johnson, principal.......... 3,339 03

July 4. By amount paid M. H. Cruikshank, President, draft in favor of Jos. H. Johnson, principal.......... 3,500 03

$7,339 02

INSTITUTION FOR THE INSTRUCTION OF THE DEAF AND DUMB IN THE UNITED STATES

	NAME.	LOCATION.	Date of Opening.	CHIEF EXECUTIVE OFFICER.	Number of Pupils in 1869.	Males.	Females.	Number of Teachers.	Mute.	Female.	Deaf Mute.	SCHOOL HOURS.
1	American Asylum,	Hartford, Conn.,	1817	Rev. Collins Stone, A. M., Principal,	279	166	113	14	8	6	6	9 to 12 and 2 to 4.
2	New York Institution,	New York, N. Y.,	1818	Isaac L. Peet, A. M., "	525	309	216	28	15	13	16	8 to 1.
3	Pennsylvania "	Philadelphia, Pa.,	1820	Abraham B. Hutton, A. M., "	218	122	96	10	9	1	3	8½ to 12½ and 2½ to 4½.
4	Kentucky "	Danville, Ky.,	1823	J. A. Jacobs, Jr., "	77	41	36	6	3	3	3	8 to 12 and 1½ to 3.
5	Ohio "	Columbus, Ohio,	1829	Gilbert O. Fay, A. M., Superintend't,	308	178	130	15	11	4	8	7½ to 9½, 10 to 12½ and 2 to 5.
6	Virginia "	Stanton, Va.,	1839	John C. Covell, A. M., Principal,	76	45	31	10	8	2	3	8½ to 1½.
7	Indiana "	Indinapolis, Ind.,	1844	Rev. Thos. MacIntire, A. M., Supt.,	224	112	102	11	8	3	5	8 to 1.
8	Tennessee School,	Knoxville, Tenn.,	1845	Joseph H. Ijams, A. B., Principal,	75	47	28	5	4	1	1	9 to 12 and 1½ to 3½.
9	North Carolina Inst.,	Raleigh, N. C.,	1845	W. J. Palmer, A. M., "	111	60	51	8	5	3	6	8 to 2.
10	Illinois "	Jacksonville, Ill.,	1846	Philip G. Gillett, A. M., "	284	141	143	14	8	6	4	8 to 12 ,
11	Georgia "	Cave Spring, Ga.,	1846	Wesley O. Connor, "	57	29	28	3	3	0	1	8 to 1.
12	South Carolina "	Cedar Spring, S. C.,	1849	(Closed).								
13	Missouri Asylum,	Fulton, Mo.,	1851	W. D. Kerr, A. M., Superintendent,	131	54	77	5	3	2	3	8 to 1.
14	Louisiana Inst.,	Baton Rouge, La.,	1852	J. A. McWhorter, A. M., "	20	8	12	2	2	0	2	9 to 12 and 1½ to 3½.
15	Wisconsin "	Delvan, Wis.,	1852	Edward C. Stone, A. M., Principal,	112	69	43	7	6	1	2	9 to 12 and 1¾ to 3¾.
16	Michigan Asylum,	Flint, Mich.,	1854	Egbert L. Bangs, A. M., "	136	78	58	9	8	1	7	8 to 12 and 1¾ to 3¾.
17	Iowa Institution,	Iowa City, Iowa,	1855	Rev. Benjamin Talbot, A. M., "	110	66	44	5	4	1	3	9 to 12 and 1½ to 3½.
18	Mississippi "	Jackson, Miss.,	1856	(Buildings burned in 1864,)								
19	Texas "	Austin, Texas,	1857	J. A. VanNostrand, A. M., "	25	19	6	3	2	1	3	9 to 12 and 1½ to 3.
20	Columbia "	Washington, D. C.,	1857	Edward M. Gallaudet, LL.D., Pres.,	119	101	18	7	6	1	1	8¼ to 12¼ and 2 to 3.
21	Alabama "	Talladega, Ala.,	1858	Joseph H. Johnson, M. D., Principal	46	16	30	2	1	1	1	8 to 1.
22	California "	San Francisco, Cal.,	1860	Warring Wilkinson, A. M., "	54	27	27	3	3	0	2	9 to 12 and 1 to 3.
23	Kansas "	Olathe, Kansas,	1862	Lewis H. Jenkins, A. M., "	35	21	14	2	1	1		9 to 12 and 1 to 3.
24	Minnesota "	Faribault, Minn.,	1863	Jonathan L. Noyes, A. M., Supt.,	55	33	22	7	2	2	1	9 to 12 and 2 to 4.
25	Clarke "	Northampton, Mass.,	1867	Miss Harriet B. Rogers, Principal,	41	24	17	5	0	5	0	Varying with age of pupil.
26	Arkansas "	Little Rock, Ark.,	1867	Marquis L. Brock, A. M., "	23	13	10	1	1	0	0	8¼ to 11½ and 2½ to 4½.
27	Maryland "	Frederick City, Md.,	1868	William D. Cooke, "	*59	41	18	3	2	1	2	*Annual Report.
28	Nebraska Institute,	Omaha, Nebraska,	1869	William M. French, "	12	6	6	1	1	0	0	9 to 12 and 2 to 4.
29	Catholic "	St. Louis, Mo.,		Mother Stanislaus, "	22	1	21	1	0	1	0	9 to 11½ and 1½ to 4.
30	Inst. for Imp'd Instr'n,	New York, N. Y.,		F. A. Rising, A. M., "	23	13	10	3	1	2	0	9 to 12 and 1 to 3.

[From American Annals of the Deaf and Dumb.]

THE ORGANIZATION OF AN INSTITUTION FOR THE DEAF AND DUMB.

———o———

BY PHILIP G. GILLETT, A. M., JACKSONVILLE, ILL.

———o———

It is not the purpose of the present paper to enter into any extended disquisition upon the importance of organization in all enterprises, but in a few pages to indicate the general principles which should underlie the organization of one of our institutions. As an army, however much of courage its assembled multitudes may add to the most scientific engineering skill and effective paraphernalia of war, without organization is but an unwieldy mob ; as a great avenue of commerce, though fully equipped for rapid and comfortable transportation of passengers and freight, without organization among its managers and employes, becomes but a wasteful agency of destruction, confusion and death ; as a commercial enterprise, however extensive its scope and ample its means, without organization results only in bankruptcy, dishonor and ruin, so one of our institutions, however profoundly learned the members of its corps of instruction, however expert its presiding officer in financial affairs, or experienced in methods of instruction, however salubrious its site, however commodious its buildings and extensive its pecuniary resources, furnishing the best possible libraries and apparatus, without systematic organization, not only fails to fulfill the ends contemplated in its establishment, but will inevitably produce some pernicious results in the character, and habits of thought of its beneficiaries. It consequently becomes the question of first importance, *what is the best plan of organizing an institution for the education of the deaf and dumb?*

The proper organization of an institution for deaf-mutes, in its moral aspects, is of more gravity than the organization of any other educational enterprise, because, by reason of their infirmity the institution is largely their world. It is here that in the years of childhood, the most impressible season of life, they are subjected to the influences of a well or an illy regulated family, influences that with other children are expressed in the tenderest words of our language, *mother* and *home.* It is here that in youth are first inspired longing anticipations for the future, and the energies that shall courageously meet its conflicts or quail in their presence. Whether the resolutions now formed shall be ennobling and such as to dignify their possessor, or such as shall tend to vagrancy, is determined more by the silent continuous influences of daily life, than by the instruction, lecture and admonition of the chapel and school-room. In nature those influences are the most powerful, and lasting in their results, which are silent and continuous. Though intellectual vigor and mental culture may be most promoted under the instructor, character is more the fruit of association and circumstances. The worst influences, to which plastic mind can be exposed, are the dissensions which result from the inharmonious relations of those about it.

We may be aided somewhat in arriving at a correct solution of our inquiry, by considering the scope of such an institution. The act of incorporation of one of our Western institutions declares: " The object of said corporation shall be to promote by all proper and feasible means, the intellectual, moral and physical culture of that unfortunate portion of the community who by the mysterious dispensation of Providence have been born, or by disease have become deaf, and of course, dumb, and by a judicious and well adapted course of education to reclaim them from their lonely and cheerless condition, restore to the rank of their species, and fit them for the social and domestic duties of life." It would perhaps be difficult to find a more correct or comprehensive statement of the purposes of one of our institutions. Education intellectual, moral and physical.

That which in other youth is effected by the family, the school, the lyceum, the lecture, the pulpit, and the innumerable other influences of society, in these is to be wrought through the agency of this single organization. It is to take them from that condition where

"Night's sable goddess sits upon her throne,
And sways her laden sceptre o'er a slumb'ring world ;
Silence how dead ! and darkness how profund !"

To elevate them to thinking, reasoning beings, who, comprehending their moral agency, may say of themselves, "a little lower than the angels." To transmute the stolid consumer into a valuable, productive member of civil society. All this must enter into the plans of those upon whom devolves the responsible task of organizing an institution for the education of the deaf and dumb. Unlike normal children, they can not look forward to a professional career, and from their infirmity, literary culture can not become advanced, before the time arrives when the acquisition of an industrial pursuit should be in progress, so that the two must be prosecuted simultaneously. Consequently, we find that our institutions are compelled to comprise an industrial as well as a literary department.

Fortunately our institutions are not private enterprises, but having their origin in the people, are supported by their benevolent impulses and are perpetual in their existence. Hence boards of trust become a necessity, and the first step in establishing such an institution is the organization of this board. Trusteeship in a deaf and dumb institution is a position of high honor and grave responsibility, yet in some respects anomalous. Those who hold this position are necessarily taken from the ordinary walks of life, and are charged with responsibilities pertaining to a profession in which it is impossible that they should be well informed. The profession of deaf-mute instruction is one as distnct and independent as any other. Indeed, there is no other profession of which so little knowledge can be gained through books, and which requires so long a practical experience to master. Men chosen from the most active pursuits, and accustomed to the management of large enterprises, as a general rule make the most efficient trustees. It is altogether a mistake to suppose that men of contemplative pursuits, of small enterprises and leisure, are best fitted for such duties. The man who has been identified with no large enterprise and is without experience in the management and control of men, is the last one to whom should be entrusted the oversight of a public institution.

The law in some of our States has provided that Trusteeship shall be a non-remunerative position, and hedged it about with provisions forbidding the pecuniary interest of trustees in the purchase of supplies or material for the institution. The later of these provisions is unquestionably wise ; the former, in view of the responsibility of the situation and the perplexities it frequently involves, is of doubtful propriety. The laborer is worthy of his hire, and he who faithfully discharges a great public trust is no less deserving of appropriate remuneration. Still the paramount consideration is not so much the individual, as the welfare of the institution, and it is not to be denied that there have been periods in the history of some of our in_stitutions when it was important that some means be devised to secure for these boards of trust, men who were actuated by a desire to serve the cause, more than by the hope of reward. This provision has the additional advantage of relieving the situation from the nature of a reward for political services, a consideration by no means trivial, as the success of an instituation imperatively demands *permanence among the officers*, of which the liability to change with political parties would be subversive. Party politics, and superdenominationalism would be the bane of any public institution. It should be a fundamental principle in the organization of every institution supported by the public, that its board of trust shall be composed as far as practicable of men who represent all the principal classes of society, who, while they are men of decision of character, never surrender themselves to partisanship.

The number composing a board of trust should be large enough to prevent its responsibilities becoming burdensome to its members, and to prevent its falling under the exclusive control of a single member. As its functions are deliberative rather than executive, the number of its members should be sufficient to **secure** a variety of opinion on subjects arising for its consideration. Yet small **enough** to insure a sense of responsibility upon all its members, and to secure the presence of a quorum at its meetings a matter of comparative ease; usually five or seven will meet these requirements.

The board of trust being organized, all authority and responsibility rests with it, and the questions at once arise to its members, what shall be the governing principles in carrying into effect the purposes of our appointment? How far shall authority be delegated to others, and what shall be reserved to the board? What officers and employees will it be necessary to secure, and how shall their relations be adjusted?

Their first and most important duty will be one which

involves more of good or ill than any other one act which
in the proper exercise of their functions they will have to
perform ; viz: the selection of the executive head of the
institution, by whatever title he may be designated. This
appointment should be made in the case of a new institution, before the location of the institution is determined or
any plans of buildings have been devised. The judgment
of the executive head of the institution in both these matters should be entertained with great weight. Thus will
the location of the institution be determined not by local
and transient causes and fixed in some remote and obscure
portion of the State, far from the majority, and out of the
reach of many for whom it is provided, and thus will the
permanent buildings have some approximation to, if not
thorough fitness for, their use. It is believed that there
are no well planned buildings for such an institution in
existence, that have not been arranged under the sugges-
tion or control of such an experienced officer ; and it is
doubted whether there has been an instance in which buildings have been erected, before the services of a principal
or superintendent were secured, that were not seriously
faulty in their adaptation to the purposes to which they
are applied. An error in the plans of permanent buildings
entails upon an institution annoyances that can not be
remedied for decades. Too much importance can not be
attached to this point, for these buildings are erected not
for a generation, but for posterity. A defect here not only
causes inconvenience, but often seriously interferes with
discipline and good order.

The trustees should as soon as practicable enact such
by-laws for the government of their own body as may be
conformable to law and expedient, and should designate
eertain *general principles* under which the management of
the institution should be conducted, holding the superin

3

dent *entirely* and *solely* responsible to them for its efficient management, making him the executive head of the institution and the organ of communication between themselves and all subordinate departments, as the agent of the *board*, though not of individual members thereof.

It will be appropriate here to name some of the characteristics to be expected in one who is called to the management of a deaf and dumb institution. There is probably no position in society that requires a greater versatility of talent and capabilities, for the perfect fulfillment of its duties. His attention must be given to matters literary, domestic, financial and mechanical, besides the enforcement of discipline, and the representation of his institution before the public ; a combination of duties so intimately associated that none of them may be separated from the other, without creating confusion and discord. It may be safely averred that such varied responsibilities do not meet in the executive officer of any other public institution. There are others under whose supervision a larger number of persons are gathered, but arduous cares are not so much multipled by an increase of the same in kind, as by the multiplication of their variety. This requires indeed a rare combination of attainments, energy, tact and equipoise of character, but one which is necessary to the discharge of the duties of the position, that there may be no clashing of departments and conflict of interest. The effort has been made to relieve the superintendent of a portion of these responsibilities by assigning them to others or retaining them to the board. Experience in this, however, has in no case been such as to commend it. On the contrary it has always proved the occasion of dissension, and a serious obstacle to every legitimate purpose of the institution. It is as unwise in principle as the appointment of two or three generals for an army, several captains for a man-of-war, or a half dozen superintendents for a railroad

It bears no analogy to co-partnership in a mercantile firm, because in that case there is community of interest, in this there is precisely the opposite. It utterly subversive of discipline, which is a *sine qua non* for the full efficiency of an educational institution, where there are not only minds, but characters of impressible nature, to learn, grow and mature.

On the efficiency and capacity of the superintendent will mainly depend the success of an institution. He should be its working man, to use a familiar expression, the mainspring and balance wheel of the establishment. Having the exclusive control of its affairs, it pertains to him to nominate and employ all persons holding subordinate positions, for thus only can harmony be secured and continuously maintained. Feeling a direct and personal responsibility, the institution becomes the subject of his thoughts, calculations, desires, hopes, in short, a part of himself. If it lacks means he will labor to create them without distraction by other engagements. He will popularize the institution in the public mind and secure it friends. He should be a man of finished classical education, of good manners and address, promptness and vigilance, and devotedly pious. He should be thoroughly versed by experience in the methods of deaf-mute instruction, and familiar with their peculiarities. He should be a good judge of human nature and have knowledge of the ways of the world. While it shall be his to govern others, he should be a good judge of human nature and have knowledge of the ways of the world. While it shall be his to govern others, he should be a man of self-control, ever ready to recognize his responsibility to the Board of Trust, and seek frequent opportunity of obtaining their counsel. His relations with the Board and its members, and especially its President, are properly of an intimate and confidential nature, and between them there should be in the interchange ef opinion, the utmost freedom. One who does not recognize his responsibility to superiors and render implicit obedience to orders. As he will have in his co-laborers, persons in intellect, attainments, social position and professional skill, fully his equals, and in some cases possibly his superiors, it will become him frequently to consult with them, and as far as practicable to have regard to their judgment in his decisions and plans.

An institution for the education of the deaf and dumb should comprise a literary, a domestic and an industrial department. In the first of these, beside the superintendent, there should be such number of professors and teachers as the perfect classification of the school requires, usually one for every eighteen or twenty pupils, but in young institutions and those having only a small number of pupils the proportion of instructors to pupils will be larger. The insrtuctors should be about equally divided between the sexes, that the pupils of each sex may have the advantage of the influence of both male and female character during their curriculum. It is altogether a perversion of the order of nature, to attempt an harmonious developement of character in either boys or girls, under the exclusive influence of either sex alone. The corps of instruction should comprise both persons who speak, and deaf-mutes, who as far as possible should be persons making this specialty their life work, for there is no other occupation among men, wherein experience is of greater value than in this, and consequently those boards act wisely, who make it their policy to employ only those who, after suitable trial, have shown themselves capable of acquiring this profession, can enter upon it *con amore*, and are willing to enter this, as men enter other professions, for life.

Among the pupils of every institution there is a very wide range of mental capacity, so that frequent modifications of existing classification is rendered necessary. This devolves upon the superintendent, to whom the duty belongs, the necessity of intimate knowledge not only with the progress of each grade of pupils, but of each pupil as well, requiring to this end frequent visitation classes. The re-classification from time to time necessary is one of the most delicate services the superintendent has to perform. The attachment between teachers, and smart, progressive, pupils is at once pleasing to witness, and natural. It is an attachment of such strength as is unknown between children who hear and speak, and their teachers. The separation of such, occasions in each a pang, that would gladly be spared did not the greatest good of the school require it. This is by no means alleviated by the fact, that the places of bright, interesting pupils, who had been promoted, are frequently supplied by others of slow, and drowsy intellect. There is naturally some feeling of discouragement with a teacher, when the labor of years is taken and passed into other hands, and to avoid this in a measure, it has been found to work well, to select from the entire school, all those pupils whose progress can only be slow, and form them into irregular classes, thus separating them from the others, and relieving the instructor, of that most perplexing and ceaseless difficulty, the proper adjustment of the relative amount of attention to be given to each quality, or grade of mind in his class. The effect upon the pupil is good, also, for those of quick perceptions and studious habits, are not retarded in their progress by those of opposite characteristics, neither are the latter discouraged by the mortification caused by the perpetual contrast between themselves and the former. The instruction of these irregular classes is the most difficult of any and requires a vast amount of patience and ingenuity in the teacher. They cannot pursue the prescribed course of study, simpler methods of teaching are required, and more repetition to advance them. Their achievements in life are not likely to bring any considerable renown to their teachers. Compared with the regular classes, these are not, by any means, inviting fields of labor, but are really those where most humane work—and, the principle of humanity is the corner stone of our profession—may be done, and in this view, these are the places of honor.

When an institution arrives at a period of its history to afford a sufficiently large number of pupils to admit of a perfect classification, the difficulty alluded to above will be largely removed, for the number of grades will be increased, and changes, when made, will not be so considerable. A word as to the number of pupils proper to be gathered into an institution may be proper here. The point is one susceptible of easy solution. All experienced teachers of deaf-mutes will agree, that eight years is as short a time as they should be in attendance upon school. The new pupils every year comprise several grades of mind, which compel at least two beginning classes—often three are desirable, but considerations of economy preclude—based upon the difference of their mental calibre. This difference continues throughout their entire course of instruction. Twenty pupils is a sufficient number for one teacher. This (20) multiplied by the number of teachers (16) which the necessities of the case, and no arbitrary decision, or dogmatic opinion renders necessary, gives us *three hundred and twenty pupils* as the proper number for an institution where the course is extended, the number should be augmented forty for each year so added. The buildings of an institution ought not to be designed in any case, for the comfortable accommodation of a smaller number than three hundred and twenty pupils, with the necessary resident officers and employees. For all these pupils, provision must be made in school-rooms, dormitories, dining-rooms, studying-rooms, lavatories, industrial departments, gymnasia and chapel. None of these can consistently be used interchangeably. Thus for each of our pupils in a thoroughly systematized building, there must be eight separate and distinct provisions made. It will thus appear obvious how extensive must be such buildings.

Monitorial service, in an institution for the education of the deaf and dumb, is one of great importance, which instructors, by reason of their permanent interest in the pupils, acquaintance with their peculiarities of character, intimate knowledge of their course of study, and appreciation of their peculiar difficulties, can perform to better purpose than any other persons. The details of this service differ in various institutions according to circumstances, but generally appertain to the oversight of pupils out of school hours, as to their deportment, cleanliness, application to study, and promptness in their allotted tasks.

Of the domestic department, the superintendent is the only proper head. He should have to aid him in this, as clerk, a man of the strictest honesty, fidelity, promptness, reliability, vigilance, reticence, and perseverance, of good business habits and experience, to whom he can safely entrust the purchase of supplies for the institution, under judicious instructions from himself, and the keeping of accounts and books. Some practical acquaintance with the management of stock, and other farm matters, will be of advantage to the individual occupying this position. The experiment has been tried of relieving the superintendent of all responsibility relative to the domestic department, by the appointment of some other officer usually called a steward. But wherever this has been done, it has been found that the functions of the position so intimately blend with others, that it operated inharmoniously, and became the occasion of estrangement and strife. In other cases, the attempt has been made to impose these labors on one of the trustees, but this has proved an *imperium in imperio*, attended by worse consequences than the former.

Of all the offices in an institution, the matron's is the most arduous, and attended by the most perplexing trials, great and small. It is also the one for which it is most difficult to find a thoroughly competent person. This is because no young person ever starts in life with the expectation of being matron of a public institution, and consequently, none undergo the preparation necessary to qualify one for these labors. We may say that good matrons, like poets, are born and not made. There is no desirable quality of the head, of the heart, or of person that is not desirable in this position, and there probably never existed an individual who possessed them all, in the exact equipoise that this situation needs. Her duties ramify every nook and corner of the institution, and bring her into communication with every person therein. She is the subject of more criticism than all others combined, and bears the sins of more people than any other purely human being. It is profitable and amusing to hear persons of opposite views, discuss the requisite traits of a matron. To sum up their views one would suppose that a matron should have a sylph-like form, combined with powers of endurance that never weary; should be queenly in her bearing, and yet know how to scrub on her knees; should grace the drawing-room, and yet be cheek-by-jowl with Bridget in the kitchen; should be able to glide around like a zephyr, and yet to bring down her foot like—thunder; should be *au fait* in the accomplishments of the French school, and yet practice chemistry over a soap-kettle; should be the most gentle and winning of creatures, and yet an inexorable administrator of discipline; that the skill of the fashionable milliner and mantua-maker should be at her fingers' ends, and yet her special delight be in patching and darning; should be redolent with "Araby's perfume" when fresh from a kettle of bacon and cabbage; that all the mysteries of the culinary art, she should thoroughly understand by experience, as well as the miseries of hard water; that in the purchase of furnishing goods, and the sale of paper rags, she should be equally exact; that the dressing of laces and linen, and the saving of scraps for bread-puddings, and soap grease, should be her constant care; that she should be a mother without children, should be able to take a little better care of every child than of any other, and allow each some privilege that no other has ever enjoyed; should have discrimination enough to perceive that the child of the mother who last visited the institution, was the smartest she had ever known. The foregoing category is only an intimation of a few of the qualities which go to make an efficient matron. When an institution is unable to secure one having them all—which is sometimes the case—it will be the part of wisdom to select one having the most substantial, for though grace and accomplishments are well enough when added to the practical ones, yet, when alone, they are but a mockery. It has been thought desirable at times to place a part of a matron's duties upon a housekeeper, but the experiment has been attended by worse results than in the case of the steward. No separation of the duties of a matron and housekeeper can be so well defined as to prevent conflict. Hence, while the matron's labors are innumerable, it is promotive of system, and order, to assign them to one person, and provide for her such assistants as she may from time to time require, giving her entire control of her assistants, with authority to change their respective duties as she may deem best.

The Industrial Department of an institution for deaf-mutes, is not of less importance than the literary, and comprises such trades as local circumstances admit of. The trades taught should be of such variety as will afford an opportunity for the tastes and proclivities of different pupils to find ample scope for their exercise. Girls are as much entitled to a living as boys, and regard should be had to their future welfare, in the organization of this department, by furnishing them a knowledge of trades which yield to them a fair return for their labor. In teaching trades to girls, care should be taken that those pursuits and domestic labors for which nature has best fitted women, are not neglected. An able report on the subject of trades for the deaf and dumb was prepared and presented to our fifth convention, in 1858, by Rev. Collins Stone, and to that reference is made, in relation to the particular branches prudent to be introduced into our institutions. The liberty is taken of quoting from that report :

"Whether the sale of the articles manufactured by the pupils can be made to equal or exceed the expense incurred in their production, we regard as a question of minor importance. The object of establishments of this character is to benefit the deaf-mute. As has been already remarked, it is to relieve him of his two-fold misfortune of ignorance ande dependence. Nor is there occasion to estimate the comparative pressure of the two ; to decide which weighs the most heavily upon him—which should be removed and which allowed to remain. He can and ought to be freed from both. The philanthropy which would teach him to labor, and leave his mind in darkness, is easily seen to be short-sighted and imperfect. Equally mistaken is the philanthrophy that would enlighten his mind, restore him to the instincts and feelings of a cultivated being, and turn him loose upon society, without means of self-support, to beg, steal, or starve, as fortune may favor him, or, at best, to become a pensioner upon the charity of others. To educate a hearing and speaking child and give him a trade, or profession by which he can support him.

self, is generally understood to involve expense. It is a heavy investment, made week by week, and year by year; for which we expect an ample return in the intelligent and productive citizen. It is the same in regard to the deaf-mute. Educate him, and give him a trade, and he becomes a worthy and intelligent member of society. To secure the true welfare of the deaf-mute, we consider both intellectual and mechanical training indispensable. And it as legitimate and proper to incur expense upon the latter as the former.

As a matter of fact, however, with a judicious selection of trades, and careful management, they can in ordinary cases be made to pay their way. More than this cannot reasonably be expected. A skillful mechanic must be employed to take charge of each branch of industry. Stock, tools, fuel and light must be provided. Then it must be remembered that a large proportion of the boys are young, averaging from twelve to fourteen years of age. Those who are older and stronger, are at first without experience.

The articles manufactured, while they may be strong and substantial, can hardly have the polish and elegance of those made by regular journeymen, and they must be sold at a cheaper rate. If the sale of the articles made will purchase the tools and stock, and pay the wages of the master mechanic, it will ordinarily evince good management, and should be satisfactory. But even if the articles produced should be given away, or their value made no account, the benefit that accrues to the pupil in their manufacture, in the practical skill and knowledge of the art acquired, would more than compensate for the expenditure incurred."

For each of the branches of industry introduced, there must be employed a skilled mechanic who is thoroughly master of his art, and also has patience and tact to teach it to apprentices.

The question of compensation has always been in our institutions one of no little annoyance. It will continue to be so until a fair remuneration is made to officers, which has not generally been done. A compensation that to a young man without dependents looking to him for support, was inviting, has been expected to support and educate a family in a style that the usages of society, and not the preference of the individual dictate. The compensation of a Professor of long experience, and marked skill, should be equal to the salaries of men of corresponding talent, in other professions somewhat analogous. It should be adequate not only to the sustenance and education of the family, but sufficient to relieve the Professor from special anxiety relative to the future, and enable him to be constantly well informed in the progress of current literature and science. The professorships in our long established and well endowed Colleges and Universities, perhaps afford as good a parallel as any other. If any amount was to be named two thousand dollars per annum would be regarded as the minimum. Had those who remain in this specialty, embarked in other professions as many former co-laborers have done, with marked success and pecuniary profit, their annual earnings would have been much more than this. There is no good reason why they should be required to spend their lives and energies upon a bare pittance in the service of the public. The people do not desire such to be the case, and it is a libel upon their justice to assert that they complain of taxation for this purpose. There is no tax that they pay so cheerfully, and there is no other object of public enterprise which the people regard with so much satisfaction and pride as the humane institutions among which ours are numbered.

The salaries of teachers cannot in all cases be uniform, but must be regulated by experience, skill, &c. Deaf and dumb teachers. have not usually been paid as large salaries as those who hear and speak. This has been partly because the supply has exceeded the demand, and partly because our courses of instruction have not been thorough enough to qualify them for the same duties. Our National College for the deaf-mutes may obviate this disadvantage and yet produce our best instructors.

Ladies have not long been in the profession, and the question of their compensation will be governed largely by the usages of society, usages which in the past have been unjust and oppressive, but which are now subjected to very extensive and able discussion.

The compensation of a clerk should be that of a first-class book-keeper, or accountant in a large mercantile firm.

The salaries of matrons will be determined much as those of lady teachers.

Masters of shops should receive the usual wages paid to foremen in similar establishments.

In fixing all salaries the principle should be distinctly recognized that valuable, skilled, and efficient service, is not to be expected without honest, just, liberal remuneration. A board of trust cannot more completely stultify itself, as to its aims and expectations, than by a parsimonious, illiberal scale of salaries.